"What we do for kicks, how we remain real
among all that steals, is why we live."

~Paul William Jacob~

Nomadic Devotion

A Contemplative Inquiry into the Poetics of Place

by

Paul William Jacob

Nomadic Devotion™ Books

Nomadic Devotion Books
P.O. Box 383
Winter Park, Florida 32792

Nomadic Devotion: A Contemplative Inquiry into the Poetics of Place
Copyright © 2016 by Paul W. Jacob
Book design by Jessica D. Jacob

First Nomadic Devotion Books trade paperback edition: December 2016.
Nomadic Devotion Books trade paperback ISBN: 978-0-9971847-0-9.

The Library of Congress has cataloged the Nomadic Devotion Books
trade paperback edition as follows:

    Jacob, Paul William.
        Nomadic Devotion / by Paul William Jacob

ISBN: 978-0-9971847-0-9

Printed in the United States of America
on recycled paper with plant-based inks.

Our books are distributed by IPG, Ingram and Baker & Taylor.

Visit us at www.nomadicdevotionbooks.com

CONTENTS

Acknowledgements

The following poems have been previously published in chapbooks/books or literary journals/magazines under my name or my pen name.

Chapbooks / Books

"Greenwich Village Trees" appeared in the chapbook *Bohemian Moss,* published by The Poets Collective, Gainesville, Florida, 1998.

"Pacific Dawn" appeared in the chapbook *Blue Moon Epiphany,* published by The Poets Collective, Gainesville, Florida, 1999.

"Portrait of Incarnation" appeared in *The Very Best of Bare Back Magazine,* published by Emerging Edge Publishing, North Carolina, 2016.

Literary Journals / Magazines

"Greenwich Village Trees", "Wyoming", and "Pacific Dawn" appeared in *Bywords Poetry* in 1998, 2011, and 2013.

"Subway" appeared in the *Café de Boheme* section of *Places Magazine* in 2002.

"Digging In" appeared in *Pudding Magazine: The Journal of Applied Poetry* in 2014.

"Craft", "Rabbit Field", and "Autumn in America" appeared in *Work Literary Magazine* in 2015.

"San Francisco Is" a.k.a. "Dharma Bridge" appeared in *First Class Lit* in 2016.

Prologue

The prose poems collected within this book are the distillation of my many years of wandering North America while developing a contemplative lens focused on the poetics of place. I chose the prose poem for its simplicity of form. I wanted the writings to be unadorned as far as elaborate line breaks and poetic devices. For me, the prose poem enabled these pieces to remain in a humble state that many readers, not just those interested in poetry, could absorb and reflect upon. It has been my experience that deep inquiry into the poetics of place can have a profound effect on our art, psyches, souls, interpersonal relationships, communities, and ultimately our cosmologies.

These writings extract the shamanic effects of place, and the subtle awakenings and transformations that took up residence within me due to deep engagement with life and contemplation of environment. This crossroads of self and setting involves things seen and unseen, people present, past and yet to arrive. This book and my spiritual practice, which I have named *Nomadic Devotion*, were formed by thousands of miles of organic discovery, spiritual longing, transient and current connections, love and loneliness, expiration and resurgence. My work is also deeply influenced by the seasonal changes of the natural world, including its diverse flora and fauna.

No matter where we live, or where we travel to, we are always in a place or moving towards or away from a place. In fact, there are two things that we can never get away from, ourselves and the place that we are in. Even in the process of traveling, we inhabit transient localities such as hotel rooms, train cars, and airplane seats. For the last twenty years of my life, I have been engaged in formal and experiential studies into the transformative nature of location. I also teach classes, give lectures, and lead holistic retreats throughout North America on "The Power of Place".

One of the foundational aspects of the holistic philosophy of *Nomadic Devotion* is that place has a profound influence on our lives. The more we can develop a deeper sense of connection to and awareness of our relation with our whole environment, the greater our ability to do authentic work within that specific vicinity, be it as a wanderer or a local.

Too many religions and spiritual systems have within their dissemination either mistrust or revulsion for the Earth which perverts the minds of its followers to seek some otherworldly, celestial, or interior palace that would be better than the place they currently inhabit. Yet, I would ask: Why are we here then? I wholeheartedly agree that human beings should cultivate a rich interior life, but do we have to forsake the external world to do this? Cannot there be synchronization between the two? I have found that a contemplative experience with the places we inhabit leads us to a deeper connection with ourselves, our community, and God-*The Beloved*.

Jesus was led into the wilderness of the desert by the spirit in order to find his true vocation by overcoming his ego, while Buddha sat under a Bodhi Tree during his supposed enlightenment. These two spiritual events did not happen in vacuums; they occurred in distinct physical places that were the ecological foundations that allowed these prophets to then venture into uncharted interior

3

lands. Ultimately, it is life here on the physical Earth that has allowed the dispersal of Christianity and Buddhism to transpire to millions of people.

The other side of the coin is the social worship of materialism that either disregards or consumes place(s) for its own ego-driven advancement and financial gain. We need look no farther than mainstream commercial real estate development and the trend of "flipping" houses as quickly as possible to see the sacred dimensions of both land and home degraded into a mass money-making contrivance.

In this techno-addicted world where scores of people are more concerned with their manufactured social media image than the rhythmic biological milieu that allows us to live here, the distinct personality and energy of actual place is being forgotten and replaced by the superficial entertainment of virtual non-places; place may one day simply become a myth to a society of people whose heads are down, eyes focused on tiny screens, and their hands forever typing on even tinier key pads: who all have no idea where they are. In other words, they are lost. This is why at the beginning of my lectures and retreats on "The Power of Place", I ask attendees a simple yet profound question: *How do you know who you are, if you don't know where you are?*

However, there is hope, as during my practice of *Nomadic Devotion* I have met and shared deeply connective time with a small, yet focused grassroots current of people from all over the world, who are striving to reawaken and keep alive the transformative aspects of the sacred and locality in their individual and collective lives. It is toward this goal that I facilitate holistically engaging community-based workshops and contemplative retreats in genuine places; for we can merge with the spirit of a location if we allow our essence and its essence to co-mingle without judgement, projection or expectation.

Mostly, I have existed on the fringes of the social order, digging into and gliding along the wandering latitudes and inner longitudes inhabited by seekers of the light, the lost, and the marginalized. I have developed a fondness for the displaced, insolvent, and overlooked, whose contributions are present in the pathways I have journeyed, the places I have inhabited, and the verses written in this volume.

For it is only those who do not fear getting misplaced physically, socially, and spiritually, who can ever truly reach *in-placement*. This veiled and drifting state is a perpetual caravan of creative sustenance, which graces the wayfarer with an individual poetic vision beyond the collective sightlessness of the mass conditioned.

The writings herein are like the feathers of a headdress, in that they come together to form a ritualistic tool that is vital for our absorption into the great emergence that roots and then resuscitates our whole self when we are ceremoniously *in place*.

The entrance to this ground of being is narrow and inaudible. Thus some of us leave nomadic tracks where and when we can.

Paul William Jacob
August 12, 2016

I dedicate this book to
all of the places
I have inhabited
along the way.

Nomadic Devotion

1

Northeast Autumnal Notes

Dusk in Rosemont
(Montreal, Canada)

A faint, mesmerizing, orange glow meanders around the stems and bodies of early green apples and pointed burgundy leaves, as the tribe of trees that encompass this place exhale solar particles back into the city atmosphere. This regenerated aura seeps onto rectangular red bricks, transforming the restored wall behind me into a cinema of arbor nuance honoring the day's end.

Abruptly, like the outstretched wings of a huge, deep purple raven returning to its cultured nest, darkness descends upon the urban wood.

My breathing is imaginary.

The clothes on the line above the tangled grapevines are marked for scarecrows.

Lion's Head Cove
(Lion's Head, Canada)

Two different species of duck families, steered by their matrons, cast their bills in and out of bright green reeds and cattails, hunting for crickets and water bugs.

A lone male Canadian goose dives into the clear shallows, his beefy hind quarters and black webbed feet extending towards easy blue sky. He hopes to catch more than the incarnate allure of shiny silver minnows navigating within a maze of pale aquatic grasses.

In the background, a stand of sugar maples soaks in the warm summer air; their fall palettes already germinating in the crisp gusts of an onshore breeze.

The Defectors
(Ottawa, Canada)

By the cover of river, flowing long mirror of time, the North Country welcomes me with its soft pace of day. Cool sun shines over my shoulder; shade maples droop over sloping bank.

An Indian path, red dirt, follows winding Ottawa River, thick blue. Ripe autumn leaves with tracing veins sail yellow and orange downstream.

Her majesty's geese go soaring over the canal, land and gather on a muddy field. After three days, the winged defectors flee. No papers, just feathers upon a southerly breeze.

The Fox and the Wildflowers
(Seneca Lake, New York)

The harvest has taken most of the grapes from the vines. Vineyards rest in deep burgundy afterglow, but the hawkeyed pilgrim can still glean unplucked charms from moseying rows with her basket in hand silent rambling through the fields.

All of creation is either pregnant or ablaze, being gathered or gazed upon, as this pagan time dances upon the earth dazzling the human psyche with a realm of bounty, magic, and infused memories.

Autumn is like a fox at the end of a hunt: enchanted with bloody game dangling from its mouth, ceremonial in the markings of its reddish brown coat, soft white underbelly stained by dirt and berries, fleet of foot, graceful and swept through memory before our pious eyes can peer into its untamed iris.

Autumn Bearer
(Tivoli, New York)

Inside of a barn tucked within the fertile Hudson River Valley, I hear the faint chimes of church bells. It is dusk on a Sunday in late September.

Leaves on rows of orchard trees shake like organic maracas after being played upon by a gust of wind. The sauntering brook below my window whispers northeast jazz into the coming night. A family of rabbits munches on tall grass along a row of blackberry bramble.

The deep blue lingering shadows of the evening sky solemnly brighten the earth, while millions of cicadas participate in their timeless chant. Dark skeletal tree arms extend out and above the softly lit barn with its warm amber fireplace glowing along the quiet country road.

Silence steeps like an herb, infusing the autumnal world with enchantment.

A train passes, whistles, journeys into dark woods beside the river.

Greenwich Village Trees
(East Village, New York City)

It is so passé, the old man's style always so grey. But that eccentric Fall Madame, in living color she dresses blowing leaves. From green boys of spring, older and bolder after repressing summer heat to autumn transvestites, seeking their first outdoor romance before the conservative, whistling winter wind sweeps the painted queens off the streets.

Garbage and Art
(Alphabet City, New York City)

Breezes drift through a community garden in Alphabet City where garbage and old toys, the objects left out by the curb, are stacked and molded together into an enormous sculpture. It is a vibrant, living work alive with the past laughter of little children, and the old memories of old people which become new again to dance and shout within the rebirth of junk.

These are the discarded treasures whose worth faded with the changing passions of their masters' fleeting Technicolor lives. This is the garbage people produced throughout their long burning years of humanity. Now, all this waste has been reshaped, reborn, and resurfaced by the imaginings of a few souls who understand how to work with garbage.

Subway
(Underground, New York City)

Fading tunes wind around the dirty subway platform, as we wait for the F train to carry our stinking bodies to the lower East Side on Saturday night.

Deeply moving clarinet melodies blow off the blistered lips of a young Hispanic kid.

Heat and filth, the rich and the filthy, are all gathered underground together inside a toxic tunnel; its dark rusted metal and cracked white tiles stained with piss and vomit.

All the good people are waiting for just the right song before their train pulls up to the platform...and they're gone.

Satori through Boston
(Lynn, Massachusetts)

I heard the ocean when I woke in your apartment this morning, peered out at the rough, unfamiliar face of the Boston seascape. Then, a day of seedy rain, many estranged faces on the subway. In a world of New England samsara, I wandered wet and hungry.

There is enlightenment in the park along Boylston, rich people walking the Theatre District.

2

Southern Spirituals

The Solace and Refinement of Heat
(Winter Park, Florida)

The fountain that had only dripped with algae-tinted water when he first bought the ramshackle place, now overflowed with the cool torrent of afternoon thunderstorms. He, like the tiles he had laid around the fountain so many years ago, had lost that shiny, superficial glow; they had evolved together through a biological weathering into something authentic, like a rock garden untouched by human hands.

His church was the falling apart old Florida courtyard, and his altar, the circular rim of the worn tile fountain where various seeds and acorns were planted in an assortment of gelato containers with handmade holes in their bottoms for the surplus water to drain. There were no other human parishioners, yet he found fellowship with the many colorful lizards that basked in the sun.

Often he contemplated the tiny red hearts of the lizards that seemed to be beating in frenzy out of the smooth white film of their chests; though the rest of their form, especially their eyes, were fixed in meditative gaze. Over time, by studying the lizards, and the vibrant green plants that thrived within this sticky environment, he too had learned to adapt and to cultivate into someone else, not a native, but a devotee of the place: someone who knew how to release passion by being motionless and breathing through the skin.

Thanksgiving Passage – Our Lady of Lourdes Convent
(St. Augustine, Florida)

The low, brittle, coquina cobbled walls do not confine the courtyard, but allow its silhouette to contemplate the form and unsettledness of God.

Crisp, brown, palm fronds knocked loose from the waving tops of slender tropical hardwood sentries, lay like battered crosses on the firm, broad grass ground.

The sisters pray inside, their silence contained within other walls, fasting while society gorges itself on habitual fare and football.

Out here, winter begins its cold, silent journey into the heart.

Still Pink Form: A Meditation on Hunger
(Tampa Bay, Florida)

Down in the mangrove, a Roseate Spoonbill Stands hunter still on what looks like one tall, thin leg. At sunrise, the spot it wades in was a spongy tan land oasis bustling with scads of minuscule side-walking black crabs.

Now, the tide is in, sheltering oysters and conch under its dull, milky, undulating late morning shimmer that flows and heightens effortlessly in between the clumped together spider-leg root stalk planted in the tepid tidewaters.

Beyond the tree line, within earshot of traffic traversing the slender I-60 isthmus of black heat-wave concrete, several marine grey dorsal fins breach the surface of the saline shallows in a playful circular formation.

All these worlds, this organic drive, occur beyond my 6th floor window: the air conditioning, smoked salmon, and jazz records.

Still, almost imperceptible among the lush tangled mangroves, its pink slender stoic form, a Roseate Spoonbill stalks the drowned oasis, waiting, for a shadow to move into the light of its hunger.

Sunday in Micanopy
(Micanopy, Florida)

On a knotty pine deck out back the farm store we sit apart, together, in the distilled sunlight fluting through the dangling fuzzy beard of embracing Spanish moss trees; and it's been a while since we've sat unrushed, breathing in still oxygen, hearing the music speak to us together, apart.

You say, "Isn't that pretty, it's raining leaves." I look up from my poem to catch greenish-yellow oblong skins twirling slow folk song rhythm down towards pumpkin blossom earth. The leaves' shiny momentary tint spray-paints nature's blue ceiling the drifting sparkle of fool's gold at the bottom of a bendy mountain stream.

As you rise to walk through the weedy garden, a breeze, with the simple power of a hundred pulsating dragonfly wings, strokes my eyelids.

Key West
(Key West, Florida)

Warm nights blow like didgeridoos, smoky indigenous melodies adhering to the skin like sticky soul salve or musty sex-soaked sheets. Rough winter transients and vacationing spirits pass one another on fast-walking, flesh-soaked Duval Street. Late night deep dream slumber under blasts of heat lightning and tropical thunder electrifying the outstretched arms of Traveler Palms with serene glow.

Subterranean black locals and early morning drunks with rough sea eyes drown in a line-up at sunrise bar. Salty dog locals bitch and beg for that years-gone-by hint of homegrown eccentricity.

There's only one bridge on and off the island of this reality.

Digging In
(Memphis, Tennessee)

In Memphis, ribs are cooked real slowly, and the Blues even slower, until the meat falls right off the bone into your soul. Like the flow of molasses being poured from a jar, heavy and sweet.

I sit in tobacco circles, listening to the digging lyrics and guitar riffs of an old black man; who, as his spirit rises to the ceiling, the roof brings him back down.

He cannot escape what makes him real.

3

Summer Elegies
from the Downeast Coast of Maine

No Bees Allowed
(The Oakland House, Brooksville, Maine)

A bee buzzes rowdily outside my bedroom window. It wants to come inside. I am drinking a cup of tea, watching the bee. Its buzzing grows louder, angry, like a fog horn exploding over a lost boat. I take another sip of tea, keep watching the bee.

Its frustration is rising, buzzing grows to agitated timbre.

The bee's pilgrim flight from the dark Maine night toward the light bulb glowing inside my third story room has come to an end at the manufactured crossroads of millions of tiny wire mesh holes.

There is something very minimal, and holy, concealed within this whole see-through scene. It reminds me of confession, or how a Taoist might dream of confession.

Wading in Sunlight
(Blue Hill, Maine)

Standing in the cool shallows of the lake, sunlight caresses our wet skin like a lone violin imparting music across the soft rippling surface of early summer lives.

We look toward the slopes of leafy shoreline hills, cajoling Mountain Ash trees to frame our portrait of blossoming love.

Wading in sunlight, the future is warm and yawning gold all around us.

Grey-Blue So
(The Oakland House, Brooksville, Maine)

Beyond the open curve of the trees lays the ocean, grey-blue lit horizon set deep into the canvas of creation. From my room I watch billions of rain drops cascading towards the summer earth. It is a good rain, a fresh bouquet of flowers, herbs and ocean drifts through the open window and settles upon my face like someone touching me gently with a scented glove.

Then there is you, light skin haloed in blue aura of evening's coming.

In the long mirror your moist body is framed like some foreign picture I have always longed to touch.

Crushed Velvet
(The Oakland House, Brooksville, Maine)

Our eyes sink into the blue and brown tapestries of each other. We talk and touch awkward, intense, through midnight hours of waking and silence.

I remember that lazy June afternoon when I watched a sun shower drift through the deep spring of your iris, transforming the color around your pupil into crushed blue velvet.

The long curvilinear shape of you makes me want to stay awake and listen to the sound of hidden rain, forever.

Red Within Them
(Penobscot Bay, Maine)

Lying in thick grass under the apple tree by the rocky beach where we first met some months ago, apples fall with symbolic thuds onto the sea of grass cushioning our entwined bodies.

Within our nervous silence during these final days of summer, the cascading fruits remind us of the time we spent together on these abandoned shores of Maine. A vanished spell that has left us bare to the natural elements of erosion, and hunger, like when high tide absconds leaving mussels and oysters exposed to birds and otters.

Observing the unripe apples, we wonder if there is red within them.

Secluded Coves of Reflection
(Little Deer Island, Maine)

It is the middle of September, and I am sitting with my bare feet hanging out the low window of a friend's cabin. The grass is long and full, deep green, speckled with yellow and purple wildflowers, smashed apples whose acrid smell permeates the surroundings, and wet silky white webs glistening amid the undergrowth.

I am thinking of you, and how we came together here in this most impossible of summers, surrounded only by water, sky, forest and mountains, intimate expanding vistas, islands in the distance.

Everything is turning from warmth to coldness, the ground, the wind, my bed, endless tides of vivid blue sea water, and remembrances of time.

The early evening light lingers in pale yellow drifts of space. Your eyes inhabit these fading pools, enduring only in secluded coves of reflection.

4

The Wyoming Poems

Wyoming
(On a ranch outside of Jackson Hole, Wyoming)

New place, new words, core breathing opens big spinal spaces, deep natural imprints inside my body like fresh moose tracks in red mud create visual representation of transient earthly being.

Horses chew dandelions in rocky sage brush pastures, while little black birds balance on top of their still, muscular, equine bodies.

Grass painted mountains meditate above raging brown snow melt river, as white peaks dissolve in the sun beyond the blooming valley.

Lazy Mountain Scenes
(On a ranch outside of Jackson Hole, Wyoming)

Sunset and dusk are cavorting, creating a sluggish pink hue over western Wyoming.

Hummingbirds dart to the sweet water feeder, insert their long pointy snouts, drink deep, and then cascade upwards in a buzzing pirouette enlivening the still crisp air with a million quick wing flaps.

The ground around the horse trailer is saturated, as the garden hose pumps chilly well water into the overflowing old tin trough. I get up from my chair planted next to the raised strawberry beds, facing the horse pasture and further bushy green mounts, and turn off the flow of irrigate at the crusty rusted spicket.

A romantic horse coupling stand by and by feeding on sage and clover, while a lovesick young stallion broods over the lone ivory mare some rocky paces away.

A fat ranch cat that I have never met before follows me back to my flatland perch. She rubs her thick tan and white coat up against my frayed and patched blue jeans.

Country Music
(On a ranch outside of Jackson Hole, Wyoming)

The long sunny Sunday is proffering its final big sheen onto the land. Two ground squirrels use their nimble paws to bend clover, dandelion and buttercup flowers down into their munching mouths.

Slim Shady (our black stallion) stands solitary in the vibrant green pasture, while his comrades lay in cool hay inside the stables. He rotates between feeding on the Kelly green grass and gazing up at the illuminated mountain clouds languishing across weightless blue sky.

There is music carrying to my cabin from somewhere in the valley. It sounds like country music.

Out here, it all is.

Autumn in America
(On a ranch outside of Jackson Hole, Wyoming))

These are the last moments of August, but summer has already left. Long days of sun and dust have turned into a chill at dusk. Soon the vivid green ground will turn brown and muddy, then frozen and packed hard under the weight of billions of distant white flakes.

The crab apple tree I transplanted in June is laden with small oblong red and yellow-skinned fruit. The young maple with its autumn-pointed salmon red and tawny-tinted leaves is bent towards the cabin, caught within the throes of the lonely Wyoming wind, as it careens and howls through screen doors and cracked windows searching for something or someone to cleave onto.

5

Northwest Draughts

We are Rivers Flowing into the Sea (for Jessica)
(Ashland, Oregon)

Inspired by the song, "Echoes of the Rogue River" by Arturo Ville

Rivers run, coursing their way through towns, valleys, and across vast meandering lands that feed our imagination with grains and music.

Our human lives diverge, crisscross, and from time to time interconnect, pouring out in medicinal harmony inside these indigenous tributaries of the unspoiled heart.

Within this native union of body and water, love is the aqueduct where our spirits gather to funnel and gush. Thunder and lightning are the organic highlights of mystical embrace; the revealing signs of lovers who ascended as one.

Craft
(Eugene, Oregon)

An old sepia photograph of blue-collar laborers hangs on the wall of a brewery in northern Oregon. The men hold, or lean into their shovels, paint and honest dirt crafting a mural of hard work on their tatty denim overalls and firm, spare, northwest immigrant faces.

Resilient orthodox spines hold red-striped suspenders in place, while their pitchforks and trowels are encrusted with a viscous mixture of caked russet mud and dried eggshell concrete that looks like spent semen.

These men were not entitled to anything, except toil, job loss, bread lines, whiskey, pungent sex, and the release of death.

Rabbit Field
(Troutdale, Oregon)

Rain drops crick down burnt yellow and washed-out green vines that creep up stone stairs, wind around black gas lanterns. The hop's acrid perfume mashes into maple, pear and grape skin gusts. Young bearded men in oilskin overalls wash the remnants of auburn suds from burnished aluminum barrels, as tanked-up craft beer tourists carouse along cropped pathways or boisterously ferment inside the bar.

A crooked, rusty water tower looms over the brunet, maize, and purple-tinted valley. It resembles an old pagan deity who stoically impregnates the deep flushed gorge.

Waterbirds
(Cortes Island, British Columbia)

In the fresh light after sunrise, two crows sit and squawk on left-handed branches of an old cedar tree above the garden.   A steady wall of mist cascades from higher atmospheres into exposed sandy soil plots of yesterday's tilled beds.

I sit at the kitchen table watching simple drops of moisture release pressure from the clouds. There is dirt under my fingernails and maple syrup in the tea.

6

The Earthquake Shaman Poems

Pacific Dawn
(Along the Great Coastal Highway, Big Sur, California)

Hollow waves break fog morning day upon the horizon. Sand and sea grass festooned by fall wind etch transient patterns into the beach. Boulders stand like stone Bodhisattvas half-drowned within the sea, unaware of duality, their silence grows deeper.

Gulls in streaking ghost flight signal eons of comings and goings echoing out of nothing.

As a young man I dreamed of the Pacific, salty shamanic dawns. Layers of atmosphere and cosmic gas surface and disperse the ethereal world.

Fresh dawn, the clean taste of new saliva swallows eternity.

Barbary Fishermen Elegy
(North Beach, San Francisco)

Ranks of wind-smacked terraced homes and apartments with their once brilliant paint jobs now wasted by salt and sun, stretch up winding hills, pray towards the harbor of this floating oceanic city.

It is evening tide, shadowy sediment surges in and out of the containers called human memory, lone glowing amber lights shine maritime existence inside thousands of planted asylums stacked haphazardly about the sinking land.

From this perch of building and time, the drowning calls of briny exposed voices sail beyond hope's chorus, too choppy and remote for any God to salvage.

Portrait of Incarnation
(Cole Valley, San Francisco)

I have no nostalgia for you. Nostalgia kisses carnal thirst
with closed lips and pretends our juicy loins do not exist.
My thoughts of you allow wood to fade, cracks in tiles,
and savor the salty balm of late afternoon sex in a small
sunlit apartment.

The kind of place where succulents ooze with sap when
their salacious bodies are squeezed and pinched, where
my appetite grows with incarnate hunger upon viewing
the slow undressing of your voluptuous Guadalajaran
portrait.

Our bodies embracing heatedly, then smoldering,
rubicund like the Pacific Sun entering deep within the
yawning western curve of earth, staining the evening sky
with ritual, and devotion.

Mission Poets
(Barrio de Mission, San Francisco)

In cozy rojo glow bars, we exist to live and rewrite our history like shadows passing through Ovid. Unannounced to the wind, we stroke upon it flimsy brushes dabbed in humanity, starkly steeped in reality.

Thorns on a vast rosebush, we sit in a garden, our tombs lying beside us.

Dharma Bridge
(Chinatown, San Francisco)

A contemporary tribute to Han Shan's "Cold Mountain"

Voices, people, dim sum carried out in steaming bamboo dishes, little pieces of food for little people with little mouths wanting nothing more than a little savory joy to chew on in the morning.

Old Chinese man plays flute on sidewalk. Soft notes float on blue skies, fall to earthen sidewalks, and these holy melancholy streets.

Wandering like a ghost through Chinatown back alleys filled with foul Orient smell, and then ascending like a ship navigating towards a lighthouse, a mountaintop seen from a distance, sun at the top of a steep hill, the Bay Bridge spanning the late afternoon horizon like a salty skeleton Buddha traversing eternity over the soft flood of karma, of connected streams and rivers and bays.

That's the way it is, San Francisco. A poem that's been written a thousand times by a thousand different voices on a thousand sheets of paper. All torn, and drowned, or folded into origami boats and set upon the sea.

Maybe one in a lifetime slips beyond the breakers, and all of the others, their dreams and hearts passionate and paddling for the big calm blue horizon, broken, flung effortlessly upon the rocky shores of our awakenings.

Epilogue

Contemplations on the Poetic Groupings in this Book

As I collected and edited the prose poems for this book, I had the wonderful opportunity to revisit these *places* from a more rooted place within myself. This reflective re-reading allowed me to garner a deeper understanding of how these locational musings were the unique expression of my budding contemplative nature and evolutionary spiritual path at those moments in my life. Now I am able to create a holistic road map of not only where I was, but of exactly what I was working through personally, socially, artistically, and spiritually within each of the six poetic groupings that appear in this book.

The first alliance is **Northeast Autumnal Notes**. I was born and raised in a highly populated area of North Jersey. Even within this urban milieu, the four seasons, especially the colorful variants of the fall, were always revealing for me. Autumn is the season of alchemy, a time that allows us to shed our conditionings and transform our selves in harmony with the natural world.

These writings celebrate the deep moments of aesthetic arrest that can work their way into our souls if we take the time to slow down and be with the biological world, as with the lines from the poem *Lion's Head Cove*, "In the background, a stand of sugar maples soaks in the warm summer air; their fall palettes already germinating in the crisp gusts of an onshore breeze." In the next poem, *The Defectors*, the difference between human rules and animal autonomy is pronounced:

> Her majesty's geese go soaring over the canal, land and gather on a muddy field. After three days, the winged

defectors flee. No papers, just feathers upon a southerly breeze.

However, what has become very clear to me is that these verses also show the dichotomy of moving from more rural or less inhabited places back into the urban population centers that I was initially more familiar with, where human nature and its inventions tend to want to obscure and dominate the animate; the tenor of my poems change from grounded moments of meditative wonder in nature to finding both concrete and metaphorical ways to bring attention to social issues such as gender roles, sexuality, political one-sidedness, materialism, and isolation within mass population. For example, the piece titled *Greenwich Village Trees* explains:

> It is so passé, the old man's style always so grey. But that eccentric Fall Madame, in living color she dresses blowing leaves. From green boys of spring, older and bolder after repressing summer heat to autumn transvestites, seeking their first outdoor romance before the conservative, whistling winter wind sweeps the painted queens off the streets.

Yet, in the last poem, *Satori through Boston*, I realize that although these settings may be different upon their surfaces, underneath both of them is simply life, like in the lines, "There is enlightenment in the park along Boylston, rich people walking the Theatre District."

In **Southern Spirituals**, regional physical environments transmute identity and consciousness, revealed in the following lines from *The Solace and Refinement of Heat*:

> He, like the tiles he had laid around the fountain so many years ago, had lost that shiny, superficial glow; they had evolved together through a biological weathering into something authentic, like a rock garden untouched by human hands.

Edifice and expanse come together in *Thanksgiving Passage* when, "The low, brittle, coquina cobbled walls do not confine the courtyard, but allow its silhouette to contemplate the form and unsettledness of God." Extensive interplay between human pathways and natural environs occurs in *Still Pink Form*:

> Beyond the tree line, within earshot of traffic traversing the slender I-60 isthmus of black heat-wave concrete, several marine grey dorsal fins breach the surface of the saline shallows in a playful circular formation.

There are also more real collisions between that raised state of understanding and the fallen, socially conditioned mind with its myriad forms of entertainment and addiction. In the poem, *Key West*, immersion is not in the bodies of water that surround this thin stretch of land but in the unconscious social current where "Rough winter transients and vacationing spirits pass one another on fast-walking, flesh-soaked Duval Street." Later in the same poem, "Subterranean black locals and early morning drunks with rough sea eyes drown in a line-up at sunrise bar."

The South has been one of the greatest training grounds with regards to helping me to release my socially constructed identity and learning to trust in my true calling and authentic self. It is the place where I learned to surf and meditate and also to engage the flesh and its passions. With the poem, *Digging In*, I come to realize that we cannot transcend what makes us existent:

> I sit in tobacco circles, listening to the digging lyrics and guitar riffs of an old black man; who, as his spirit rises to the ceiling, the roof brings him back down. He cannot escape what makes him real.

We must go through the world, not over or around it; and we certainly should never abandon it for our own private enlightenment. That Blues guitarist in Memphis was a Bodhisattva, as he proved that performing our true vocation within a genuine setting can lead to a revelation of the eternal in form.

Summer Elegies from the Downeast Coast of Maine is about love, more specifically seasonal and environmental love. And, ultimately, the loss or letting go of transient human affection to make room for a vast dimension of being that honors, reveres, and celebrates our perennial relationship with the Earth as our bourgeoning Mother. The section starts off with *No Bees Allowed*, which takes on both a physical and metaphorical tone after the whole group has been read through. I am in a new place, and at first I cannot find a way to let the bee, which plays the part of nature within the metaphor, inside of me. Slowly but surely over the course of the summer, and a summertime romance, nature begins to find her own way through "the manufactured crossroads of millions of tiny wire mesh holes" that exist in my human psyche.

The next few poems are devoted to exploring the surrounding landscape of lakes, coves, rocky beaches, and old rooms with poignant views with another seasonal worker:

> Standing in the cool shallows of the lake, sunlight caresses our wet skin like a lone violin imparting music across the soft rippling surface of early summer lives.

Finally, at the end of these Maine poems, the "you" and the "your" in the earlier pieces is no longer attached to the person that I had had a romantic relationship with, but Gaia, the Goddess of the Earth, who burned away my young passions and illusions and set my heart within her "secluded coves of reflection" within Penobscot Bay that mirror the eternal sea.

The Wyoming Poems are about a place that from the moment when I arrived, on a ranch outside of Jackson Hole to work as a chef at a camp for at-risk youth, greeted me with its arms wide open, which allowed me to breathe deep and contemplate. That's why the first poem in this collection is named *Wyoming*, and says, "New place, new words, core breathing opens big spinal spaces..." Not only does Wyoming offer vast environmental room, but it also allows me to inhale into all of those interior locations that I could not feel in Portland (Oregon, where I had moved to Wyoming from).

I revel in "the long sunny Sunday" and "weightless blue sky" up on that plateau, and also hear the "country music" that permeates the ranch and mountain air. The last poem, *Autumn in America*, signifies the end to this enchantment, and the fact that once again I must move on from a place of learning, from all that I have physically and psychologically planted there, to continue on my journey because "summer has already left" and "soon the vivid green ground will turn brown and muddy, then frozen and packed hard under the weight of billions of distant white flakes." Yet what I have learned from Wyoming will remain with me.

Northwest Draughts is only four poems long, but what these pieces bring together, more effortlessly than anywhere else in this book, are the Hindu spiritual concepts of karma yoga (work) and jnana yoga (wisdom). When we do our true work on the deepest level, without yearning for admiration, financial security, or insurance of any kind, we finally come into contact with our foundational being, which allows us to labor with love. In order to understand karma yoga, one must also realize that many people have toiled under harsh conditions, as the poem *Craft* points out:

> An old sepia photograph of blue-collar laborers hangs on the wall of a brewery in northern Oregon. The men hold, or lean into their shovels, paint and honest dirt crafting a mural of hard work on their tatty denim overalls and firm, spare, northwest immigrant faces.

However, in the next poem titled *Rabbit Field*:

> A crooked, rusty water tower looms over the brunet, maize, and purple-tinted valley. It resembles an old pagan deity who stoically impregnates the deep flushed gorge.

Like in the philosophy of the *Tao Te Ching*, the great symbolic work that is being accomplished here is done through perfect inaction. Eventually, in the piece *Waterbirds,* karma yoga and jnana yoga come to fruition through a meditative scene:

> In the fresh light after sunrise, two crows sit and squawk on left-handed branches of an old cedar tree above the garden. A steady wall of mist cascades from higher atmospheres into exposed sandy soil plots of yesterday's tilled beds.

> I sit at the kitchen table watching simple drops of moisture release pressure from the clouds. There is dirt under my fingernails and maple syrup in the tea.

It is no mistake that the final sequence of this work is devoted to Northern California, mostly San Francisco, and is entitled **The Earthquake Shaman Poems.** Perhaps no other place brought me into direct confrontation with the shadow side of myself, as its "Ranks of wind-smacked terraced homes and apartments with their once brilliant paint jobs now wasted by salt and sun, stretch up winding hills, pray towards the harbor of this floating oceanic city."

My body, psyche, and soul lived with a daily onslaught of ungrounded spiritual ideologies and New Age sensations, cataclysmic personal and social financial menstruations, and innate, locationally-charged shamanic teachings that forced me to look at myself without malice or sympathy, and ultimately to transform my life. That is much easier to admit now, but when we are in it, "From this perch of building and time, the drowning calls of briny exposed voices sail beyond hope's chorus, too choppy and remote for any God to salvage," as stated in *Barbary Fishermen Elegy*.

But it is exactly this drowning that allows the wayfarer to learn how to swim on their own, to rise up beyond the squishy, unripe philosophies of the spiritual materialists and capitalistic artists to say, "I have no nostalgia for you. Nostalgia kisses carnal thirst with closed lips and pretends our juicy loins do not exist." This same lack of reminiscence from *Portrait of Incarnation* is again indicated in *Mission Poets* with these brief lines, "Thorns on a vast rosebush, we sit in a garden, our tombs lying beside us."

Beyond the tasteless rational dialectic morality of academic philosophers and theologians, and the deludedness of irrational personal power mantra harbingers, exists *The Beloved* playing hide and go seek with creation. Only when we fully enter into this Maya or play of life, can we possibly cross the "salty skeleton Buddha traversing eternity over the soft flood of karma," like in the book's final poem *Dharma Bridge*. Or, can we be without fear and trepidation when we read that poem's ending lines:

Maybe one in a lifetime slips beyond the breakers, and all of the others, their dreams and hearts passionate and paddling for the big calm blue horizon, broken, flung effortlessly upon the rocky shores of our awakenings.

We will never know how we shall fair against the waves if we never paddle out to surf in an ocean; its expansive marine body may be near or far away from the place where we are now.

~Fin~

THE AUTHOR

Paul William Jacob is originally from North Jersey. He is a writer, poet, teacher, and contemplative guide. Jacob facilitates spiritual retreats at centers of consciousness across the United States. He was also the Co-Founder and Publishing Director of the culturally influential *Modern Nomad* magazine. Jacob has been a featured guest on several regional NPR programs and college radio shows, where he talks about the poetics of place, transformative travel, and alternative media.

Jacob currently teaches writing and spiritual/religious classes at select colleges in Florida and for several retirement centers. He has had numerous spiritual essays, travel stories, and poems published in cultural magazines and literary journals. He also collaborated with the late great jazz pianist Eddie Higgins on the poetry and jazz album, *Miami Session*.